A Benjamin Blog
and His Inquisitive Dog
Guide

France

Anita Ganeri

Heinemann
LIBRARY

Chicago, Illinois

© 2015 Heinemann Library
an imprint of Capstone Global Library, LLC
Chicago, Illinois

Edited by Dan Nunn, Helen Cox Cannons,
and Gina Kammer
Designed by Jo Hinton-Malivoire
Picture research by Ruth Blair and Hannah Taylor
Production by Helen McCreath
Originated by Capstone Global Library Ltd
Printed and bound in China by Leo Paper Group

18 17 16 15 14
10 9 8 7 6 5 4 3 2 1

Library of Congress
Cataloging-in-Publication Data
Cataloging-in-publication information is on file with
the Library of Congress.
ISBN 978-1-4109-6667-4 (hardcover)
ISBN 978-1-4109-6676-6 (paperback)
ISBN 978-1-4109-6694-0 (eBook PDF)

Acknowledgments
We would like to thank the following for permission
to reproduce photographs:

Alamy: Action Plus Sports Images, 22, Angelo
Hornak, 12, Carlo Bollo, 15, Directphoto.org,
17, Jean-Yves Roure, 14, John Kellerman, 4,
LatitudeStock, 23, Oleksii Sergieiev, 7; Getty
Images: AFP/Lionel Bonaventure, 18, Bloomberg/
Caroline Blumberg, 25, M G Therin Weise, 11,
Sylvain Sonnet, 16, Visions of America/Joseph
Sohm, 10; Shutterstock: Gurgen Bakhshetsyan, 13,
Iakov Kalinin, cover, Kiev.Victor, 6, macumazahn, 8,
Neirfy, 27, Paul Stringer, 28, PHB.cz/Richard Semik,
9, Prochasson Frederic, 21, WDG Photo, 26, 29;
Superstock: age fotostock/J.D. Dallet, 24, Robert
Harding Picture Library, 19, Tips Images/Dino
Fracchia, 20

Some words are shown in bold, **like this**. You can find
out what they mean by looking in the glossary.

Contents

Welcome to France! 4

Palaces and Statues 6

Mountains, Rivers, and Beaches 8

Big Cities 12

Bonjour! 14

Lunchtime 20

Taking a Break 22

From Farms to Factories 24

And Finally 26

France Fact File 28

France Quiz .29

Glossary 30

Find Out More 31

Index 32

Welcome to France!

Hello! My name is Benjamin Blog and this is Barko Polo, my **inquisitive** dog. (He is named after ancient ace explorer, **Marco Polo**.) We have just gotten back from our latest adventure—exploring France. We put this book together from some of the blog posts we wrote on the way.

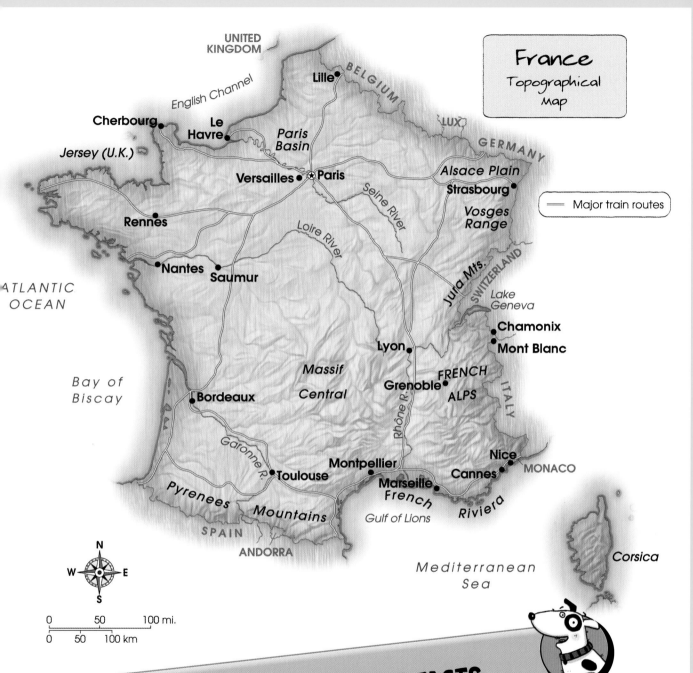

France
Topographical
Map

UNITED KINGDOM

English Channel

Lille

BELGIUM

LUX.

GERMANY

Cherbourg

Le Havre

Paris Basin

Alsace Plain

Strasbourg

Jersey (U.K.)

Versailles • ☆ Paris

Seine River

Vosges Range

Major train routes

Rennes

Loire River

Jura Mts.

SWITZERLAND

Lake Geneva

ATLANTIC OCEAN

Nantes • Saumur

Chamonix

Mont Blanc

Bay of Biscay

Massif Central

Lyon

FRENCH

Bordeaux

Grenoble

Rhône R.

ALPS

ITALY

Garonne R.

Montpellier

Nice

MONACO

Toulouse

Marseille

Cannes

Pyrenees

French

SPAIN

Mountains

Gulf of Lions

Riviera

ANDORRA

Mediterranean Sea

Corsica

N W E S

0   50   100 mi.
0   50   100 km

BARKO'S BLOG-TASTIC FRANCE FACTS

France is a large country in Europe. It has coastlines with the English Channel, Atlantic Ocean, and Mediterranean Sea. On land, it is joined to Spain, Italy, Switzerland, Germany, Luxembourg, Belgium, Andorra, and Monaco.

Palaces and Statues

Posted by: Ben Blog | March 31 at 11:45 a.m.

The first stop on our tour is the magnificent Palace of Versailles outside Paris. It was first built by King Louis XIII, who ruled France from 1643 to 1715. It was later changed into a palace by King Louis XIV. Now it has more than 2,000 rooms, so it is easy to get lost. I sent Barko off to find a guide.

BARKO'S BLOG-TASTIC FRANCE FACTS

Napoleon Bonaparte was a brilliant army general who made himself **emperor** of France in 1804. However, he was beaten by the British in 1815 at the Battle of Waterloo. No wonder this statue of Napoleon looks so cross!

Mountains, Rivers, and Beaches

Posted by: Ben Blog | April 14 at 7:56 a.m.

From Versailles, we headed to the Alps to climb Mont Blanc. It is the highest mountain in France at 15,771 feet (4,807 meters). If you do not like climbing, you can always go skiing or walking at the nearby town of Chamonix instead.

BARKO'S BLOG-TASTIC FRANCE FACTS

The Loire is the longest river in France. It flows for 634 miles (1,020 kilometers), from the Massif Central mountains to the Atlantic Ocean. It is famous for its **châteaux**, like this one at Saumur.

After a hard day's climbing, we needed a rest, so we traveled south for a little sunbathing. This stretch of coast is called the French Riviera, and it is famous for its sunny weather and sandy beaches. There are also beaches and sensational **sand dunes** along the west coast.

BARKO'S BLOG-TASTIC FRANCE FACTS
The Camargue is a huge **marsh** in the south of France, where the Rhône River flows into the sea. It is home to hundreds of birds, including pink flamingos, as well as herds of wild horses and bulls.

Big Cities

Posted by: Ben Blog | May 3 at 11:49 a.m.

Our next stop was Paris, the capital city of France. It is famous for the Notre Dame Cathedral, the Arc de Triomphe, the Louvre museum, and lots more besides. The best way to get around is by subway, which is known as the Métro. Now, I just need to figure out which train to catch!

BARKO'S BLOG-TASTIC FRANCE FACTS

Marseilles is France's second biggest city and its main **port**. Each year, millions of tons of goods, such as oil, chemicals, plastics, and olive oil, pass through the busy port.

13

Bonjour!

Posted by: Ben Blog | May 5 at 11:23 a.m.

While we are here, I am trying to learn some French. It is going quite well so far. *Bonjour* means "hello" and *au revoir* means "good-bye." "*Je m'appelle Benjamin Blog. C'est mon chien, Barko,*" means "My name is Benjamin Blog. This is my dog, Barko."

BARKO'S BLOG-TASTIC FRANCE FACTS

Some countries in Africa were once ruled by France. Many people from these countries have come to live in France. These women are wearing traditional African scarves and clothing.

In France, children have to go to school between the ages of 6 and 16. These children are at an *école* (primary school). When they are 11, they go to a *collège* (middle school). Then, at 15, they move on to a *lycée* (high school). Older children sometimes go to school on Saturday mornings too!

BARKO'S BLOG-TASTIC FRANCE FACTS

Many French people live in apartments in cities. Some apartment buildings, such as this one, are very old. In many cities, high-rise buildings and skyscrapers are not allowed.

Well, we are back in Paris for Bastille Day. It is a national holiday, and everyone is out celebrating. On July 14, 1789, an angry crowd attacked the Bastille prison in Paris. They were tired of being hungry and poor while the king lived in luxury. Afterward, France got rid of the king and became a **republic**.

BARKO'S BLOG-TASTIC FRANCE FACTS

Many French people are **Roman Catholics**. There are also many **Muslims**. Many come from countries in North Africa that were once ruled by France.

Lunchtime

Posted by: Ben Blog | July 16 at 1:15 p.m.

French food is famous all over the world, so we treated ourselves to lunch in a café. France is especially famous for its **pâté**, cooked meats, and cheese. People shop in supermarkets but also in local markets for fruits and vegetables.

BARKO'S BLOG-TASTIC FRANCE FACTS

I popped into this **boulangerie** to buy a loaf of bread. These long loaves are called **baguettes**. They are crispy on the outside and chewy inside. Delicious!

Taking a Break

Posted by: Ben Blog | July 28 at 10:02 a.m.

Here in Provence, we are watching the Tour de France. It is one of the most popular sporting events in France. Around 200 cyclists take part in the race, which lasts for 23 days and covers about 2,000 miles (3,200 kilometers). The leader wears a yellow jersey—that's him now.

BARKO'S BLOG-TASTIC FRANCE FACTS

Boules is a game that is played all over France. The aim is to get your boule (ball) as close as possible to a smaller ball, called the cochonnet (jack). For some reason, the players get really annoyed if I run off with any of the balls!

From Farms to Factories

Posted by: Ben Blog | August 2 at 4:36 p.m.

These **vineyards** in Bordeaux grow grapes, which are made into wine. French wine is world famous, and about 8 billion bottles are produced each year. Farmers also grow fruit, wheat, olives, and sunflowers. They keep sheep, pigs, and chickens. Some raise cattle for their meat and milk.

AIRBUS

BARKO'S BLOG-TASTIC FRANCE FACTS

Thousands of French people work in high-tech factories. This factory in Toulouse builds the Airbus 380—the world's largest airplane. French factories also produce around 131,000 cars every month.

And Finally ...

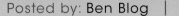

For the last stop on our trip, it was back to Paris. Here is a photo that Barko took of me in front of the amazing Eiffel Tower. It was built in 1889 from around 10,000 tons of steel. The tower is 1,063 feet (324 meters) tall, and I am taking the elevator to the third level for a breathtaking view of the city.

BARKO'S BLOG-TASTIC FRANCE FACTS

The beautiful **Château** of Chambord stands by the Loire River. It is around 500 years old. It is famous for its double, spiral staircase—one person can walk up and one person can walk down without meeting on the way.

France Fact File

Area: 212,935 square miles
(551,500 square kilometers)

Population: 65,951,600 (2013)

Capital city: Paris

Other main cities: Marseilles; Lyon; Lille

Language: French

Main religion: Christianity (Roman Catholic)

Highest mountain: Mont Blanc
(15,771 feet/4,807 meters)

Longest river: Loire
(634 miles/1,020 kilometers)

Currency: Euro

France Quiz

Find out how much you know about France with our quick quiz.

1. How do you say "hello" in French?
a) *au revoir*
b) *bonsoir*
c) *bonjour*

2. Which is the highest mountain in France?
a) Mont Blanc
b) Mount Everest
c) Mount Vesuvius

3. What is a **baguette**?
a) a loaf of bread
b) a type of sausage
c) a hat

4. What type of race is the Tour de France?
a) running
b) motor
c) cycling

5. What is this?

Glossary

baguette a long loaf of French bread

boulangerie a French word for a bakery

château a French castle, often found along the Loire River

emperor a ruler

inquisitive being interested in learning about the world

Marco Polo explorer who lived from about 1254 to 1324; he traveled from Italy to China

marsh flooded land, often around the edges of lakes

Muslim a person who follows the religion of Islam

pâté a paste made from meat

port a town or city next to a river or the sea, where ships load and unload goods

republic a country ruled by a president who is elected by the people

Roman Catholic a Christian who belongs to the Roman Catholic Church

sand dune a giant heap of sand, piled up by the wind

vineyard a place where grapes are grown for making into wine

Find Out More

Books

Bedoyere, Camilla De La. *France in Our World* (Countries in Our World).
Mankato, Minn.: Smart Apple Media, 2011

Powell, Jillian. *Looking at France* (Looking at Countries).
Milwaukee: Gareth Stevens Pub., 2007

Savery, Annabel. *France* (Been There!).
Mankato, Minn.: Smart Apple Media, 2012

Websites

kids.nationalgeographic.com/kids/places
The National Geographic website has lots of information, photos, and maps of countries around the world.

www.worldatlas.com
Packed with information about various countries, this website includes flags, time zones, facts, maps, and timelines.

Index

Africa 15, 19
Airbus 25
Alps 8
Arc de Triomphe 12
Atlantic Ocean 5, 9
Bastille Day 18
Battle of Waterloo 7
Belgium 5
Bonaparte, Napoleon 7
Bordeaux 24
boules 23
Camargue 11
Chamonix 8
Château of Chambord 27
châteaux 9, 27
Eiffel Tower 26, 29
emperor 7
English Channel 5
Europe 5
euros 28
food 20, 21, 24, 29
French 14, 28, 29
French Riviera 10
Germany 5
Italy 5
King Louis XIII 6
King Louis XIV 6

Lille 28
Loire River 9, 27, 28
Louvre 12
Luxembourg 5
Lyon 28
Marseilles 13, 28
Massif Central mountains 9
Mediterranean Sea 5
Métro 12
Mont Blanc 8, 28, 29
Muslim 19, 30
Notre Dame Cathedral 12
Palace of Versailles 6
Paris 6, 12, 18, 26, 28
Polo, Marco 4
ports 13
Provence 22
republic 18
Rhône River 11
Roman Catholic 19, 28
Saumur 9
schools 16
Spain 5
Switzerland 5
Toulouse 25
Tour de France 22, 29
Versailles 6, 8

2932